Psychology
A Level Paper 3

Forensic psychology

The Complete Companion Exam Workbook

Name

OXFORD

OXFORD
UNIVERSITY PRESS

Great Clarendon Street, Oxford, OX2 6DP, United Kingdom

Oxford University Press is a department of the University of Oxford.
It furthers the University's objective of excellence in research, scholarship, and education
by publishing worldwide. Oxford is a registered trade mark of Oxford University Press in the
UK and in certain other countries

British Library Cataloguing in Publication Data
Data available

978-0-19-842893-0

7 9 10 8 6

Paper used in the production of this book is a natural, recyclable product made from wood
grown in sustainable forests. The manufacturing process conforms to the environmental
regulations of the country of origin.

Printed in Great Britain by Ashford Colour Press

Acknowledgements

The publishers would like to thank the following for permissions to use their photographs:

Cover: all images from Shutterstock.

Photos: all images from Shutterstock.

Although we have made every effort to trace and contact all copyright holders before
publication this has not been possible in all cases. If notified, the publisher will rectify any
errors or omissions at the earliest opportunity.

Contents

Introduction

The Complete Companions series of psychology textbooks were originally devised to provide everything that students would need to do well in their exams. Having produced *The Complete Companion Student Books*, the *Mini Companions*, and the *Revision and Exam Companions*, the next logical step was to produce a series of *Exam Workbooks* to provide a more hands-on experience for psychology students throughout their course and particularly in the period leading up to the exam.

Each of the *Exam Workbooks* in this series is focused on one particular exam. This book covers the topic of Forensic Psychology (Paper 3: Section D). Each two-page spread of psychology in the Student Book has an equivalent set of exam questions and advice in this Exam Workbook. It is designed for you to write in, so that you gain valuable experience of constructing responses to a range of different exam questions.

A distinctive feature of this *Exam Workbook* is the 'scaffolding' that we provide to help you produce effective exam answers. The concept of scaffolding is borrowed from the field of developmental psychology, where it is a metaphor describing the role of more knowledgeable individuals in guiding children's learning and development. Our scaffolding takes the form of providing sentence starters and exam tips for most questions, to help you develop the skill of writing effective exam answers. All of the material used in our scaffolding comes from the Student Book, and you are provided with page references for that book so that you can find the right material to complete the answer.

Guide to your A Level Paper 3 exam (Issues and options in psychology)

This paper contains four sections, each worth 24 marks. Section A is compulsory. For Sections B–D, you choose one topic (e.g. for Section D you choose either Aggression or Forensic Psychology or Addiction) and answer all the questions on that particular topic.

The content of the four sections is as below:

Section A
Issues and debates in psychology

All questions in this section are compulsory. Questions may focus on any of the Issues detailed in the specification (e.g. gender and cultural bias, ethical issues) or Debates (e.g. free will and determinism, the nature-nurture debate, holism and reductionism). There will be a mixture of low (e.g. 1, 2, 3 marks) and high tariff (e.g. 8, 16) marks and also a mixture of AO1 (selection, description), AO2 (application) and AO3 (evaluation) questions. Not all topics will appear in the exam but you need to revise them all as they are all equally likely to appear.

Section B
Relationships; Gender; Cognition and development

You (or more probably your teacher) will have chosen one of these topics to study. Questions can be set on any of the different aspects of these topics that are detailed in the specification (e.g. for 'Gender', questions might focus on measuring androgyny, including the Bem Sex Role Inventory, psychodynamic explanations of gender development, gender identity disorder etc.). There will be a mix of low and high tariff marks and a mixture of AO1, AO2 and AO3 questions.

Section C
Schizophrenia; Eating behaviour; Stress

In this Section, you will have chosen to study schizophrenia, eating behaviour or stress. Questions can be set on any of the different aspects of these topics that are detailed in the specification (for 'Schizophrenia', e.g. questions might focus on the classification of schizophrenia, biological and psychological explanations, token economies in the treatment of schizophrenia etc.). As with Sections A and B, there will be a mix of low and high tariff marks and a mixture of AO1, AO2 and AO3 questions.

Section D
Aggression; Forensic psychology; Addiction

As with Sections B and C, you will have chosen one of these topics to study. As this workbook is about Forensic Psychology, then it is likely that this is the topic you are studying. Again, there will be a mix of low and high tariff marks and a mixture of AO1, AO2 and AO3 questions.

The total mark for this paper will be 96 marks and you will have two hours to answer four questions (one from each Section).

How to use this Exam Workbook

Specification notes

Each spread begins with the AQA specification entry for this particular topic. This tells you what you need to learn and drives the questions that might be asked in your exam.

Student Book page reference

Each spread has a reminder of the pages where you can read about this topic in **The Complete Companion Year 2 Student Book**.

Topic links

Sometimes you will find a link between the topic on a particular spread to something in the Student Book that we feel will enhance your understanding of that topic. This might be a further discussion of the topic itself, the methods used in its investigation, or anything else that we feel might be useful to develop your understanding of that topic.

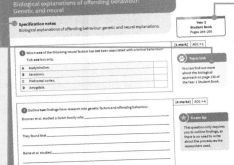

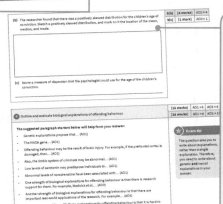

Questions

On each spread we have given you some sample exam questions. These give you experience of questions related to a particular topic area. This is not an exhaustive list of all the possible questions you could be asked on this topic, but it gives you the opportunity to practise answering the most common form of questions.

Mark box

Exam questions have different mark 'tariffs', suggesting how much you should write in response. We have tried to help you with this by giving you an appropriate number of lines in which you can fit your answer. Questions may also be AO1 (description), AO2 (application), or AO3 (evaluation), which will indicate what particular approach you should take in your response.

Scaffolding

A key feature of this Exam Workbook is that for most questions we have provided some 'scaffolding' to help you construct an effective response to the question. This scaffolding takes the form of sentence starters or appropriate links between points. You can then flesh out this material to make a full answer.

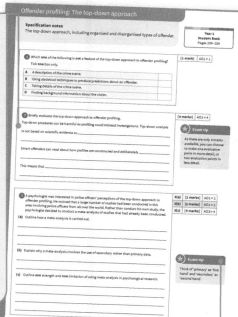

Sample answers

In some topics you will find an answer already provided. We have provided complete answers to some questions to give you some idea of the appropriate level and length of response necessary to gain full marks.

Exam tips

There are a number of helpful exam tips throughout the Exam Workbook. Sometimes these are general pieces of advice (e.g. the importance of elaborating AO3 points for maximum impact). At other times they are specific guidance about how to answer a particular question, or how to avoid common mistakes when answering that question.

Essay question

We have included scaffolding for the AO1 and AO3 components of the 16 mark essay questions. We have usually included five AO3 points, although you may choose to use four of these in greater detail.

Types of A Level exam question

Question type	Example	Advice

Simple selection/ recognition	*Which* **one** *of the following best describes the differential association theory of offending behaviour?* (1 mark)
	
	  A *Criminal behaviour is inherited rather than learned.*
	
	  B *Criminal behaviour is an interaction between biological and social factors.*
	
	  C *Criminal behaviour is a result of socialisation.*
	
	  D *Criminal behaviour is a result of an underdeveloped superego.*
	
	Which **one** *of the following is* **not** *a feature of the top-down approach to offender profiling?* (1 mark)
	
	  A *A description of the crime scene.*
	
	  B *Using statistical techniques to produce predictions about an offender.*
	
	  C *Taking details of the crime scene.*
	
	  D *Finding background information about the victim.*
		Questions such as these should be straightforward enough, so the trick is making sure you have selected the right answer to gain maximum marks. If you aren't sure which answer is the right one, try crossing through those that are obviously wrong, thus narrowing down your options. For example, in the first question on the left, answer **D** uses a psychodynamic concept (superego), so that can be crossed out. Likewise, question **A** is describing genetic explanations, so that narrows down the correct answer to either **B** or **C**. Note also that sometimes (as in the second question on the left), the question requires you to identify which statement is incorrect (e.g. is **not** a feature of), so careful reading is vital.

Description questions (e.g. Describe, Outline, Identify, and Name)	*Describe the psychodynamic explanation of offending behaviour.* (6 marks) *Outline* **two** *findings from research into genetic factors and offending behavior.* (4 marks) *Explain Eysenck's theory of the criminal personality.* (4 marks) *Name a measure of dispersion that the psychologist could use for the age of the children's conviction.* (1 mark)	To judge how much to write in response to a question, simply look at the number of marks available and allow about 25 words per mark. If the sole command word is 'Name' or 'Identify', there is no need to develop a 25 word per mark response, simply identifying or naming (as required by the question) is enough. These questions may have a variety of tariffs (e.g. 2, 3, 4 marks), so you need to tailor the amount of information you give to the number of marks being awarded. Don't give more than is necessary (e.g. in response to the third question) and don't miss out on the extra marks available by not giving *enough* content (e.g. in response to the first question).
Differences/Distinguish between	*Distinguish between the top-down and bottom-up approaches to offender profiling.* (3 marks) *The HIT-Q is both reliable and valid. Explain the difference between the reliability and validity of a psychological test.* (2 marks)	You might be tempted to ignore the instruction to 'distinguish between' and simply outline the two terms or concepts named in the question. This is not what is required, and would not gain credit. Words such as 'whereas' and 'however' are good linking words to illustrate a difference between two things.
Applying knowledge	*A residential neighbourhood experienced a number of arson attacks, which always occurred in the early morning. There were no witnesses to the attacks, and very little physical evidence for the police to go on.* *Using your knowledge of the bottom-up approach to offender profiling, explain how geographical profiling could be used to help the police in the item described above.* (4 marks) *Ian was an uncooperative prison inmate, and refused to take part in any organised activities. The only thing prison officers knew about Ian was that he really liked seeing Liverpool play football. However, he couldn't do this in prison as the inmates were not allowed to watch television.* *Using information in the item above, outline how behaviour modification might be used to increase Ian's cooperativeness.* (4 marks)	In these AO2 questions, you will be provided with a scenario (the question 'stem') and asked to use your psychological knowledge to provide an informed answer. You must make sure that your answer contains not only appropriate psychological content, but that this is set explicitly within the context outlined in the question stem. For example, in the second question on the left, you are not just being asked to describe how behaviour modification is used, but how it might be used to change Ian's uncooperative behaviour.

Types of A Level exam question (cont)

Research methods questions	You will be given a description of a study and then a number of short questions such as: (a) *What level of measurement is being used in this study?* (1 mark) (b) *Identify the type of experimental design used by the researcher in this study and outline one limitation of this type of experimental design.* (3 marks) (c) *The researcher found that the difference between the scores for the offenders and non-offenders was significant at $p < 0.05$. What is meant by 'the difference was significant at $p < 0.05$'?* (2 marks) (d) *Calculate the mean and median extraversion scores for the sample used in this study.* (2 marks) (e) *Identify the type of experimental design used by the researcher in this study, and outline one advantage of this type of experimental design.* (3 marks) (f) *Falsifiability is an important feature of science. Explain why it is important that hypotheses derived from psychodynamic theories are falsifiable.* (3 marks)	Most (but not all) research methods questions are set within the context of a hypothetical research study. This means that your answers must also be set within the context of that study. If you don't set your answers within the specific context of the study, you cannot receive full marks. Question (e) is a classic example of this. You are not being asked why falsifiability is such an important feature of science but why, specifically, it is so important in the context of psychodynamic hypotheses of offending behaviour
Maths questions	(a) *What percentage of children did not have a criminal conviction by the age of 18? Show your calculations.* (2 marks) (b) *The researcher found that there was a positively skewed distribution for the children's age of conviction. Sketch a positively skewed distribution, and mark on it the location of the mean, median, and mode.* (3 marks)	'Maths' questions can appear anywhere on the paper, and can assess your ability to carry out simple calculations, construct graphs, and interpret data, e.g. in the first question, a correct answer and an explanation of how you arrived at this number are necessary for maximum marks.
Evaluation questions	*Briefly evaluate the top-down approach to offender profiling.* (4 marks) *Explain **one** criticism of using behaviour modification as a way to deal with offender behaviour.* (4 marks) *Evaluate cognitive distortions as an explanation for offending behaviour.* (4 marks) *Evaluate the bottom-up approach to offender profiling.* (6 marks)	It is important that you elaborate your evaluative points for maximum marks. We have shown you how to achieve this through the 'scaffolding' feature. With questions worth 2, 3 or 4 marks, you could choose one elaborated critical point, but with 6 mark questions (such as the 4th question on the left), you would usually include two elaborated critical points in your answer.
Mixed description and evaluation questions	*Briefly outline and evaluate psychodynamic explanations of offending behaviour.* (6 marks) *Briefly explain anger management as a way of dealing with offender behavior, and give **one** limitation of this approach.* (6 marks)	Not all questions are straightforward 'description only' or 'evaluation only', but may be mixed. As a rule of thumb, in questions like these you should divide your AO1 and AO3 content equally.
Extended writing questions	*Outline and evaluate cognitive explanations of offending behaviour.* (12 marks) *Discuss custodial sentencing as a way of dealing with offending behaviour.* (16 marks) *Discuss restorative justice programmes.* (16 marks) *As part of a national conference for prison officers, delegates were asked to discuss what, in their experience, was the most effective way to deal with persistent offenders in order to prevent them offending again. Some of the opinions expressed are summarised in the table below.* <table><tr><td>**Table 1**</td></tr><tr><td>Allow prisoners to meet their victims and to understand the consequences of their crime.</td></tr><tr><td>Teach prisoners different ways in which they might deal with their anger.</td></tr><tr><td>Reward prisoners with treats (e.g. extra TV) when they behave well and withdraw treats when they misbehave.</td></tr></table> *Discuss **one or more** ways of dealing with offending behaviour. Refer to some of the suggestions in your answer.* (16 marks)	As a rough guide, 300–360 words would be appropriate for an answer to a 12-mark question and 400-500 words for a 16-mark question. As there are more marks allocated to AO3 than AO1, then your response should contain more AO3 than AO1 content. If the command word is 'Discuss', you should go a bit deeper in your AO3, possibly looking at both sides of an argument or considering the implications or applications of the topic being discussed. An increasingly common type of extended writing question is the type that includes a scenario (or stem) as in the final question opposite. In a 16-mark question, four marks are assigned to your analysis of the stem material in the context of the main topic (in this case ways of dealing with offending behaviour). It is easy to miss this, so keep your eyes open!

The way your answers are marked

Questions and mark schemes

Examiners mark your answers using mark schemes and marking criteria. These vary from question to question, depending on the specific demands, but below are some examples.

1-mark questions: 1 mark is given for an accurate selection of the right answer or an appropriate identification. Giving the wrong answer or selecting more than one alternative from those available would result in 0 marks.

2-mark questions: For questions such as '*The researcher could have used an independent groups design in her study, but chose to use a matched pairs design instead. Suggest one reason why she might have made this decision*', and '*Explain one limitation of the sampling technique used in this study*', a little elaboration is necessary to push your answer up from 1 mark to 2 marks. Other 2-mark questions such as '*What percentage of children did not have a criminal conviction by the age of 18? Show your calculations*' have two requirements (i.e. the correct answer and appropriate workings), which would receive 1 mark each.

3-mark questions: These questions might focus on a descriptive point, e.g. '*Briefly explain restorative justice programmes as a way of dealing with offending*', where the mark awarded would reflect the detail, accuracy, and overall organisation of your answer. They can also be evaluative, e.g. '*Give **one** limitation of the restorative justice programmes*'. The number of marks awarded in these AO3 questions is largely determined by the degree of elaboration of your critical point.

4-mark questions: Descriptive and evaluative questions can sometimes be assigned 4 marks, so will require slightly more detail or elaboration than you would write for a 3-mark question. It is useful to try to write the same number of 'points' as the marks available. You may be familiar with the PEEL (Point, Evidence, Explanation, Link) approach that involves making four different statements for a 4-mark AO3 question. Sometimes 4-mark questions are simply two 2-mark questions in disguise, i.e. they contain two specific components, each worth 2 marks.

6-mark questions: These can have very different requirements (e.g. description only, description plus application, or evaluation only), in which case their actual wording varies, e.g. you may come across a question such as '*Describe differential association theory as an explanation of offending behaviour*' (6 marks) or '*Briefly outline and evaluate the historical approach as a way of explaining offending behaviour*' (6 marks). For each of these you need to decide what is an appropriate level of breadth (e.g. how many descriptive points for each of these questions, how many evaluative points for the second question) and depth (how much detail, how much elaboration).

8-, 12-, and 16-mark questions: Questions above 6 marks are generally referred to as 'extended writing' questions. They always have more than one requirement, so examiners will be assessing (usually) both AO1 and AO3 in what is effectively a short essay response. There are four main criteria that an examiner will be looking for in extended writing answers.

Description (AO1) – have you described the material accurately and added appropriate detail? There are a number of ways in which you can add detail. These include expanding your description by going a bit deeper (i.e. giving more information rather than offering a superficial overview), providing an appropriate example to illustrate the point being made, or adding a study (which adds authority and evidence of wider reading).

Discussion/ Evaluation (AO3) – have you used your critical points effectively? Examiners will be assessing whether you have made the most of a critical point. A simple way is to identify the point (e.g. that there is research support), justify the point (e.g. provide the findings that back up your claim) and elaborate the point (e.g. link back to the thing being evaluated, demonstrate how research support strengthens a theory or adds support to a research study). In this Exam Workbook we have aimed at writing 30 words of evaluation per mark available for AO3.

- A Level 8-mark question = up to 5 marks for AO3 and so around 150 words of evaluation, or 3 marks for AO3, if there are marks awarded for AO2, and so around 90 words for AO3

- 12-mark question = 6 marks for AO3 and so 180 words of evaluation

- 16-mark question = we have worked on the assumption that you would use five AO3 points of 60 words each. However, you might decide to just use four of the AO3 points we provide and expand each to 75 words. This is entirely appropriate.

Remember, if the command word is '*Discuss*' rather than '*Outline and evaluate*', your AO3 should be more discursive in nature. This might involve looking at both sides of an argument, considering the consequences of a particular critical point and so on.

Organisation – does your answer flow and are your arguments clear and presented in a logical manner? This is where planning pays off as you can organise a structure to your answer before you start writing. This is always more effective than just sticking stuff down as it occurs to you!

Specialist terminology – have you used the right psychological terms (giving evidence that you have actually understood what you have read or been taught) rather than presented your material in lay (i.e. non-specialist) language? This does not mean you have to write in an overly formal manner. Students often mistakenly believe that they have to use the sorts of words that they would never use in everyday life!

How do examiners work out the right mark for an answer?

Mark schemes are broken down into different levels. Each of these levels has a descriptor, which describes what an answer for that level should look like, i.e. an average performance for that range of marks. Lower levels have less demanding descriptors, and frequently make use of criteria such as 'lacking detail', 'many inaccuracies', and 'poorly organised'. Examiners must first decide on the right level for your response. To do this, they start at the lowest level to see whether the answer meets (or exceeds) the descriptor for that level. If it meets the criteria for the lowest level, the examiner moves up to the next level, and so on, until they have a match between the level descriptor and the answer.

Answers

All answers for this Exam Workbook can be found at:

www.oxfordsecondary.co.uk/completecompanionsanswers

Offender profiling: The top-down approach

Specification notes
The top-down approach, including organised and disorganised types of offender.

> **Year 2**
> **Student Book**
> Pages 258–259

[1 mark] | **AO1 = 1**

1 Which **one** of the following is **not** a feature of the top-down approach to offender profiling?

Tick **one** box only.

A	A description of the crime scene.	
B	Using statistical techniques to produce predictions about an offender.	
C	Taking details of the crime scene.	
D	Finding background information about the victim.	

[4 marks] | **AO3 = 4**

2 Briefly evaluate the top-down approach to offender profiling.

Top-down processes can be harmful as profiling could mislead investigations. Top-down analysis

is not based on scientific evidence so _____

_____

Smart offenders can read about how profiles are constructed and deliberately _____

_____

This means that _____

_____

> ⭐ **Exam tip**
>
> As there are only 4 marks available, you can choose to make one evaluative point in more detail, or two evaluation points in less detail.

[4 marks] | **AO1 = 4**

3 Distinguish between organised and disorganised types of offender.

Organised offenders tend to be _____

_____

and commit crimes which are _____

_____

Disorganised offenders on the other hand tend to be _____

_____

and leave crime scenes which are _____

_____

4 A research team wanted to evaluate the impact of victimisation on victims of various crime types. They used a mixed methods approach, including both quantitative and qualitative data collection. Over 3000 people who had agreed to be contacted for the purposes of the research were invited to complete an online questionnaire asking structured questions about the impact of crime. Of these, 390 people from all over England and Wales took part. The researchers also conducted in-depth unstructured interviews with people who had been victims of crime. These explored how the experience of crime had affected their lives.

4(a)	[2 marks]	AO1 = 2
4(b)	[2 marks]	AO2 = 2
4(c)	[2 marks]	AO3 = 2
4(d)	[2 marks]	AO2 = 2

(a) Explain the difference between quantitative and qualitative data.

_____

_____

(b) Suggest **one** reason why the findings from this study might not be representative of people who are victims of crime.

_____

_____

(c) The study used unstructured interviews to explore how the experience of crime had affected people's lives. Outline **one** strength of this method of data collection.

_____

_____

(d) The research team wanted to conduct a thematic analysis of their interview recordings. Suggest a reason why they might have wanted to do this.

_____

_____

Exam tip

Research methods can be assessed in all of your examinations, so be prepared for them popping up anywhere!

Exam tip

Thematic analysis is a technique used when analysing qualitative data. Themes or categories are identified and then data is organised according to those themes.

---

5 A psychologist was interested in police officers' perceptions of the top-down approach to offender profiling. He noticed that a large number of studies had been conducted in this area involving police officers from all over the world. Rather than conduct his own study, the psychologist decided to conduct a meta-analysis of studies that had already been conducted.

3(a)	[2 marks]	AO1 = 2
3(b)	[2 marks]	AO1 = 2
3(c)	[4 marks]	AO3 = 4

(a) Outline how a meta-analysis is carried out.

_____

_____

_____

(b) Explain why a meta-analysis involves the use of secondary rather than primary data.

_____

_____

(c) Outline **one** strength and **one** limitation of using meta-analysis in psychological research.

_____

_____

_____

_____

Exam tip

Think of 'primary' as 'first hand' and 'secondary' as 'second hand'.

	[12 marks]	AO1 = 6	AO3 = 6
6 Outline and evaluate the top-down approach to offender profiling.	[16 marks]	AO1 = 6	AO3 = 10

The suggested paragraph starters below will help form your answer:

- The top-down approach to offender profiling starts from a general classification of the crime scene, then… (AO1)

- This method relies on… (AO1)

- Data is collected, including a detailed description of the crime scene and… (AO1)

- Decision process models are created. This is… (AO1)

- The crime is classified as being committed by an organised, or disorganised, offender. An organised offender is… (AO1)

- A disorganised offender is… (AO1)

- One strength of top-down profiling is that it can be useful for opening up new lines of inquiry. For example, Copson… (AO3)

- However, one limitation of top-down profiling is that it may not be accurate. For example, Alison *et al.*… (AO3)

- A second limitation of top-down profiling is that the data on which the organised/disorganised classification is based may be flawed. For example… (AO3)

- Another limitation of top-down profiling is that the distinction between an organised and disorganised offender may not be true. For example, Canter *et al.*… (AO3)

- A final limitation of top-down approaches is that they can be harmful as profiling could mislead investigations. For example… (AO3)

Exam tip

This question requires you to show both your AO1 skills ('outline') and your AO3 skills ('evaluate'). If the question is worth 12 marks, then the AO1 and AO3 marks on offer are the same. However, if the question is worth 16 marks, more marks are awarded for showing your AO3 skills.

Offender profiling: The bottom-up approach

Specification notes
The bottom-up approach, including investigative psychology; geographical profiling.

---

1 Which **one** of the following is **not** a feature of investigative psychology? [1 mark] AO1 = 1

Tick **one** box only.

A	Smallest space analysis.	
B	Forensic awareness.	
C	Interpersonal coherence.	
D	Geographical profiling.	

---

2 Briefly evaluate the bottom-up approach to offender profiling. [4 marks] AO3 = 4

One limitation of the bottom-up approach is that circle theory has been criticised.

For example, Canter and Larkin studied 45 sexual assaults and found that _____

_____

However, in cities, _____

_____

This means that _____

_____

---

3 A residential neighbourhood experienced a number of arson attacks, which always occurred in the early morning. There were no witnesses to the attacks, and very little physical evidence for the police to go on. [4 marks] AO2 = 4

Using your knowledge of the bottom-up approach to offender profiling, explain how geographical profiling could be used to help the police in the item described above.

Geographical profiling analyses _____

A 'marauder' commits crimes that are _____

_____

However, 'commuters' will _____

_____

It is likely that these crimes were committed by a _____

_____

This would help the police by _____

_____

> ⭐ **Exam tip**
>
> Remember that on questions like these, it is vital that your answer is contextualised.

4 Police forces use several different geographic profiling models, such as DRAGNET and ROGEL. All models have been used successfully in police investigations, but anecdotal evidence from police officers suggest that some are easier to use than others. A researcher devised two new geographic profiling models, and decided to test these for their ease of use with 20 police officers. The officers received training on the methods in a counterbalanced way, and then rated them according to how easy they found them to use. The researcher's first model was rated significantly easier to use than his second model.

4(a)	[3 marks]	AO2 = 1	AO3 = ₂
4(b)	[2 marks]	AO2 = 2	
4(c)	[4 marks]	AO2 = 4	

(a) Identify the type of experimental design used by the researcher in this study, and outline **one** advantage of this type of experimental design.

_____

_____

_____

 Exam tip

Ask yourself – how were the participants allocated to the conditions in this investigation, and why is this better than allocating them in some other way?

(b) The researcher used counterbalancing in his study. Explain why it was necessary to do this.

_____

_____

(c) Identify a statistical test that was appropriate to use to analyse the data in this study, and give **three** reasons why this test is appropriate.

_____

_____

_____

_____

	[12 marks]	AO1 = 6	AO3 = 6

5 Outline and evaluate the bottom-up approach to offender profiling.

	[16 marks]	AO1 = 6	AO3 = 10

The suggested paragraph starters below will help form your answer:

- The bottom-up approach is a data-driven method in which statistical techniques are used to… (AO1)

- There are three main features of this approach. They are… (AO1)

- Geographical profiling involves… (AO1)

- Circle theory says… (AO1)

- Criminal geographic targeting is… (AO1)

- One strength of the bottom-up approach is that it has a scientific basis. For example, it uses… (AO3)

- Another strength of this approach is that investigative psychology can be useful. For example, Copson… (AO3)

- However, one limitation of the bottom-up approach is that circle theory may be flawed. For example, Petherick… (AO3)

- Another limitation of the bottom-up approach is that geographical profiling is limited to spatial behaviour. For example, it ignores… (AO3)

- A final limitation of the bottom-up approach is that offender profiling should be used with caution. This is because… (AO3)

Exam tip

Evaluation is not limited to the suggestions offered here. You could use your knowledge of the top-down approach and its strengths and limitations to evaluate the bottom-up approach!

Biological explanations of offending behaviour: A historical approach

Specification notes
Biological explanations of offending behaviour: a historical approach (atavistic form).

Year 2
Student Book
Pages 262–263

1 Which **one** of the following is **not** a view associated with the atavistic form explanation of offending behaviour?

[1 mark] AO1 = 1

Tick **one** box only.

A	Criminals possess similar characteristics to lower primates.	
B	People's innate physiological make-up causes them to become a criminal.	
C	Some people are born with a criminal personality.	
D	Criminals have symmetrical faces.	

2 Outline the historical approach to explaining offending behaviour. Refer to atavistic form in your answer.

[4 marks] AO1 = 4

Lombroso proposed that offenders possess characteristics that are similar to _____

_____

He identified three types of criminal. These are _____

_____

He gathered empirical evidence from _____

_____

Sheldon linked body types to temperaments. For example, _____

_____

> ⭐ **Exam tip**
>
> The specification names 'atavistic form' as an example of the historical approach, but there are other historical approaches to offending behaviour you could write about.

3 According to a recent newspaper article, scientists believe that it might be possible to identify a criminal by looking at their face. Researchers have developed software that they claim can be used to identify a person who has committed a crime with up to 89.5 per cent accuracy.

[4 marks] AO2 = 2 AO3 = 2

Use your knowledge of the atavistic form to briefly evaluate the claim made by the researchers in the above item.

Lombroso's research had no controls, so _____

_____

If controls had been used, Lombroso would have found _____

_____

This means that the researchers' claim is incorrect, because _____

_____

4(a)	[2 marks]	AO2 = 2
4(b)	[4 marks]	AO2 = 4
4(c)	[2 marks]	AO2 = 2
4(d)	[1 mark]	AO2 = 1
4(e)	[1 mark]	AO2 = 1

4 Lombroso argued that if criminality was inherited, then 'born criminals' could be distinguished by physical atavistic 'stigmata' such as high cheekbones, handle-shaped ears, and insensitivity to pain. A researcher decided to test the hypothesis that criminals have a higher pain tolerance than non-criminals. She matched ten men who had at least one criminal conviction with ten men none of whom had criminal convictions. She found that those with a criminal conviction could keep a hand in an ice water container for a mean time of 165 seconds, whilst those with no criminal conviction could keep a hand immersed for a mean time of 151 seconds.

(a) The researcher could have used an independent groups design in her study, but chose to use a matched pairs design instead. Suggest **one** reason why she might have made this decision.

_____

_____

(b) Outline **one** ethical issue raised by this study, and suggest **one** way in which it could have been dealt with.

_____

_____

_____

_____

Exam tip

Ethical issues include confidentiality, deception, informed consent, privacy, protection from harm, and right to withdraw.

(c) Suggest **one** disadvantage of using the mean as a measure of central tendency in this study.

_____

_____

(d) Name a measure of dispersion the researcher could have used in this study.

_____

(e) Suggest an appropriate statistical test that could be used to analyse the difference between the two groups of participants in this study.

_____

	[12 marks]	AO1 = 6		AO3 = 6
	[16 marks]	AO1 = 6		AO3 = 10

5 Discuss the historical approach to explaining offending behaviour.

The suggested paragraph starters below will help form your answer:

- Lombroso proposed that offenders possess characteristics that are similar to… (AO1)

- He identified three types of criminal. These are… (AO1)

- He gathered empirical evidence from… (AO1)

- Sheldon linked body types to temperaments. For example… (AO1)

- One strength of the historical approach is that Lombroso's research looks scientific. For example, it used… (AO3)

- Another strength of the historical approach is that there is some research support for somatotypes. For example, Glueck and Glueck… (AO3)

- However, one problem with the historical approach is that it is gender biased. For example, Lombroso… (AO3)

- Another problem with the historical approach is that it is deterministic. For example… (AO3)

- However, although the theory of atavistic form has been discredited, we still try to identify criminal types. For example, Eysenck's theory… (AO3)

_____

Exam tip

'Discuss' is a command word which requires you to show both your AO1 and AO3 skills. You'll need to show your knowledge and understanding of the historical approach **and** be able to evaluate it!

Biological explanations of offending behaviour: Genetic and neural

Specification notes
Biological explanations of offending behaviour: genetic and neural explanations.

Year 2
Student Book
Pages 264–265

---

1 Which **one** of the following neural factors has **not** been associated with criminal behaviour?

[1 mark] | AO1 = 1

Tick **one** box only.

A	Acetylcholine.	
B	Serotonin.	
C	Prefrontal cortex.	
D	Amygdala.	

Topic link

You can find out more about the biological approach on page 132 of the Year 1 Student Book.

---

2 Outline **two** findings from research into genetic factors and offending behaviour.

[4 marks] | AO1 = 4

Brunner *et al.* studied a Dutch family who _____

_____

They found that _____

_____

Raine *et al.* studied _____

_____

They found that _____

_____

Exam tip

This question only requires you to outline findings, so there is no need to write about the procedures the researchers used.

---

3 A researcher studied criminality in 1500 children who had been adopted by parents who did not themselves have a criminal record. He found that 330 of those whose biological parents had a criminal record had been convicted of a criminal offence by the age of 18. The modal age when the children were convicted was 13.

3(a) | **[2 marks]** | AO2 = 2

(a) What percentage of children did not have a criminal conviction by the age of 18? Show your calculations.

_____

_____

Exam tip

You should ensure that you fully understand the difference between the three measures of central tendency. The 'mode' is the most frequently occurring score in a data set.

(b) The researcher found that there was a positively skewed distribution for the children's age of conviction. Sketch a positively skewed distribution, and mark on it the location of the mean, median, and mode.

| 3(b) | [4 marks] | AO2 = 4 |
| 3(c) | [1 mark] | AO2 = 1 |

(c) Name a measure of dispersion that the psychologist could use for the age of the children's conviction.

_____

---

4 Outline and evaluate biological explanations of offending behaviour.

| [12 marks] | AO1 = 6 | AO3 = 6 |
| [16 marks] | AO1 = 6 | AO3 = 10 |

The suggested paragraph starters below will help form your answer:

- Genetic explanations propose that… (AO1)

- The MAOA gene… (AO1)

- Offending behaviour may be the result of brain injury. For example, if the prefrontal cortex is damaged, then… (AO1)

- Also, the limbic system of criminals may be abnormal… (AO1)

- Low levels of serotonin may predispose individuals to… (AO1)

- Abnormal levels of noradrenaline have been associated with… (AO1)

- One strength of biological explanations for offending behaviour is that there is research support for them. For example, Mednick *et al.*… (AO3)

- Another strength of biological explanations for offending behaviour is that there are important real-world applications of the research. For example… (AO3)

- However, one problem with these explanations for offending behaviour is that it is hard to link them to non-violent crimes. For example… (AO3)

- Another problem with biological explanations is that they are deterministic. For example… (AO3)

- A final problem with biological explanations for offending behaviour is that a lot of the research is based on studies with non-human animals. This means that… (AO3)

_____

_____

_____

_____

_____

_____

_____

_____

Psychological explanations of offending behaviour: Eysenck's theory

Specification notes
Psychological explanations of offending behaviour: Eysenck's theory of the criminal personality.

Year 2
Student Book
Pages 266–267

---

1 Which **one** of the following is **not** a feature of Eysenck's theory of the criminal personality?

Tick **one** box only.

A	Personality traits have a biological basis.	
B	The link between personality and criminal behaviour can be explained in terms of arousal.	
C	The environment does not play a role in the development of criminality.	
D	There are three major dimensions of personality.	

[1 mark] AO1 = 1

 Exam tip

As always, it is important to read the question very carefully. Without careful reading you might miss the word '**not**' in this question, and then mistakenly choose an answer that *is* a feature of Eysenck's theory.

---

2 Explain Eysenck's theory of the criminal personality.

Eysenck's theory says that character traits cluster along three normally distributed dimensions.

These are _____

_____

Extroverts will seek out more arousal and therefore _____

_____

Neurotics are unstable, and so may _____

_____

Psychotic individuals lack _____

_____

[4 marks] AO1 = 4

 Exam tip

Remember to make your answer specific to the 'criminal personality' rather than just describing Eysenck's views on personality generally.

---

3 Wayne is a young man whose friends are worried by his apparent inability to understand and share other people's feelings. John's friends are worried by some of the dangerous things he does when they are out together, such as playing 'chicken' at a railway crossing. Pete's friends are worried by his tendency to overreact in potentially threatening situations.

Using your knowledge of Eysenck's theory, identify the personality types shown by Wayne, John, and Pete. Justify your answer.

_____

_____

_____

_____

_____

_____

_____

[6 marks] AO2 = 6

 Exam tip

Don't forget to refer to the scenario when you justify your choice of personality for each individual.

_____

_____

_____

_____

4(a)	[3 marks]	AO2 = 1	AO3 = 2
4(b)	[4 marks]	AO2 = 4	
4(c)	[2 marks]	AO1 = 2	

4 Several studies have looked at personality differences in offenders and non-offenders. A researcher conducted a small-scale study in which ten first-time violent offenders were compared with ten non-offenders in terms of their scores on the Psychoticism scale of Eysenck's Personality Questionnaire. She carried out a statistical test on the results, and found that the offenders did have a significantly higher mean score than the non-offenders. The difference was significant at $p < 0.05$.

(a) Identify the type of experimental design used by the researcher in this study, and outline **one** disadvantage of this type of experimental design.

_____

_____

_____

(b) Identify a statistical test that was appropriate to use to analyse the data in this study, and give **three** reasons why this test is appropriate.

_____

_____

_____

_____

 Exam tip

Is the researcher looking for a difference or correlation? How have participants been allocated to conditions? What level of measurement has been used?

(c) The researcher found that the difference between the scores for the offenders and non-offenders was significant at $p < 0.05$. What is meant by 'the difference was significant at $p < 0.05$'?

_____

_____

5 Discuss Eysenck's theory of the criminal personality.	**[12 marks]**	AO1 = 6	AO3 = 6
	[16 marks]	AO1 = 6	AO3 = 10

The suggested paragraph starters below will help form your answer:

*   Eysenck's theory says character traits cluster along three normally distributed dimensions. These are… (AO1)

*   Extroverts will seek out more arousal and therefore… (AO1)

*   Neurotics are unstable, and so may… (AO1)

*   Psychotic individuals lack… (AO1)

*   One strength of this explanation of offending behaviour is that there is research support for personality types. For example, Zuckerman… (AO3)

*   Another strength of this explanation of offending behaviour is that there is research support for a link between personality traits and criminal behaviour. For example, Dunlop *et al.*… (AO3)

*   A third strength is that personality trait theory may have real-world applications. For example… (AO3)

*   However, one criticism of this explanation is that personality tests lack validity. For example… (AO3)

*   Another criticism of personality trait theory is that it assumes personality is consistent. For example… (AO3)

_____

_____

_____

_____

_____

_____

_____

_____

_____

_____

_____

_____

_____

_____

_____

_____

_____

_____

_____

_____

_____

_____

_____

Psychological explanations of offending behaviour: Cognitive

Specification notes

Psychological explanations of offending behaviour: cognitive explanations; level of moral reasoning and cognitive distortions, including hostile attribution bias and minimalisation.

Year 2
Student Book
Pages 268–269

---

1 Which **one** of the following is **not** a feature of cognitive explanations of offending behaviour?

[1 mark] AO1 = 1

Tick **one** box only.

A	Hostile attribution bias.	
B	Epigenetics.	
C	Minimalisation.	
D	Levels of moral reasoning.	

---

2 Evaluate cognitive distortions as an explanation for offending behaviour.

[4 marks] AO3 = 4

One strength of the cognitive distortions explanation is that there is research support for hostile attribution bias.

For example, Schönenberg and Aiste showed participants _____

_____

They found that _____

_____

This might explain _____

_____

⭐ **Exam tip**

This question is AO3 only, so there is no need to provide an outline of the cognitive distortions explanation.

---

3 Charlie and Alan were discussing the circumstances in which they might commit a crime. 'I might break the law if I was certain I was going to get away with it,' said Charlie. 'I wouldn't,' said Alan. 'I'd only ever break the law if I had to protect a member of my family.'

[6 marks] AO1 = 3 AO2 = 3

Identify the levels of Kohlberg's moral reasoning theory shown by Charlie and Alan, and outline the features of these levels.

Charlie is _____

People at this level of moral reasoning think _____

_____

Alan is _____

People at this level of moral reasoning think _____

_____

4 One reliable and valid way of measuring cognitive distortions is the 'How I Think Questionnaire' (HIT-Q). This consists of 54 items measuring four categories of self-serving cognitive distortions. In one study, researchers found a significant positive correlation between the number of offences committed by juvenile offenders and their scores on the category that measures the extent to which anti-social behaviour is seen as causing no real harm or as being acceptable and even admirable.

4(a)	[2 marks]	AO1 = 2
4(b)	[2 marks]	AO2 = 2
4(c)	[2 marks]	AO2 = 2
4(d)	[2 marks]	AO2 = 2

(a) The HIT-Q is both reliable and valid. Explain the difference between the reliability and validity of a psychological test.

_____

_____

(b) Sketch a scattergram of the relationship between the two variables in the study described in the item above.

Exam tip

The item will give you all the information you need to determine what kind of relationship your scattergram should show.

(c) Explain what is meant by the term concurrent validity.

_____

_____

(d) Outline **one** way in which the concurrent validity of the HIT-Q could be assessed.

_____

_____

_____

5 Outline and evaluate cognitive explanations of offending behaviour.

[12 marks]	AO1 = 6	AO3 = 6
[16 marks]	AO1 = 6	AO3 = 10

The suggested paragraph starters below will help form your answer:

* Cognitive explanations of offending behaviour focus on… (AO1)

* One type of cognitive distortion is hostile attribution bias. This is… (AO1)

* Another type of cognitive distortion is minimalisation. This is… (AO1)

* Kohlberg's theory of moral reasoning says that… (AO1)

* The level of moral reasoning that criminals are more likely to be at is… (AO1)

* One strength of cognitive explanations of offending behaviour is that there is research support for hostile attribution bias. For example, Schönenberg and Aiste… (AO3)

* Another strength of cognitive explanations is that there is research support for minimalisation. For example, Kennedy and Grubin… (AO3)

* A third strength of cognitive explanations of offending behaviour is that they have real-world applications. For example… (AO3)

Exam tip

The question asks you to write about cognitive explanations, rather than a single cognitive explanation. Therefore, you need to write about **at least two** cognitive explanations in your answer.

- One strength of Kohlberg's theory is that there is research support for it. For example, Gudjonsson and Sigurdsson… (AO3)

- However, one problem with Kohlberg's theory is that it concerns moral thinking, not behaviour. For example… (AO3)

_____
_____
_____
_____
_____
_____
_____
_____
_____
_____
_____
_____
_____
_____
_____
_____
_____
_____
_____
_____
_____
_____
_____
_____
_____
_____
_____
_____
_____
_____

Psychological explanations of offending behaviour: Differential association

Specification notes
Psychological explanations of offending behaviour: differential association theory.

Year 2
Student Book
Pages 270–271

---

1 Which **one** of the following best describes the differential association theory of offending behaviour?

[1 mark]   AO1 = 1

Tick **one** box only.

A	Criminal behaviour is inherited rather than learned.	
B	Criminal behaviour is an interaction between biological and social factors.	
C	Criminal behaviour is a result of socialisation.	
D	Criminal behaviour is a result of an underdeveloped superego.	

---

2 Outline differential association as an explanation of offending behaviour.

[4 marks]   AO1 = 4

Sutherland proposed that offending behaviour can be explained by social learning theory. The

child learns _____

They learn this from _____

_____

The degree of influence these social associations have is determined by _____

_____

   Exam tip

Remember that 'Outline' questions are AO1 only, so resist the temptation to evaluate differential association as an explanation of offending behaviour.

---

3 Researchers interested in computer piracy sent an email to 500 students. Students were asked to indicate whether or not they downloaded music files without paying for them. They were also asked whether or not their closest friends engaged in the same activity. There were 320 students who replied to the email. The results are summarised below:

3(a)   [4 marks]   AO2 = 4

	I download music files illegally	I do not download music files illegally
My closest friends download music files illegally	127	34
My closest friends do not download music files illegally	22	137

(a) Outline **one** potential ethical issue in the study described above, and suggest **one** way in which it could have been dealt with.

_____

_____

_____

_____

_____

(b) Explain **one** limitation of the sampling technique used in this study.

_____

_____

_____

(c) What level of measurement is being used in this study?

_____

(d) Name an appropriate statistical test that could be used to analyse the data in this study.

_____

3(b)	[2 marks]	AO2 = 2
3(c)	[1 mark]	AO2 = 1
3(d)	[1 mark]	AO2 = 1

 Exam tip

There is no need to explain why you have named a particular test.

---

4 Differential association theory has both supporters and critics. Supporters point to the findings from research studies and its explanatory power. Critics, however, argue that its explanatory power is limited, that it concentrates only on social factors, and that research into it is methodologically limited.

Using **at least one** of the claims made above, evaluate differential association theory as an explanation of offending behaviour.

| **[10 marks]** | AO2 = 4 | AO3 = 6 |

 Exam tip

You must refer to **at least one** of the claims made about differential association theory in your answer if you want to gain full marks on this question.

The suggested paragraph starters below will help form your answer:

- One strength of differential association as an explanation for offending behaviour is that there is research support for it. For example, Osborn and West… (AO3)

- Another strength of differential association is that this theory has made a major contribution to understanding the causes of crime. For example… (AO3)

- However, one problem with this explanation is that it may explain only some types of crime. For example… (AO3)

- Another problem with differential association as an explanation for offending behaviour is that it ignores biological factors. For example… (AO3)

- A final problem with differential association is that the research is correlational. It is possible that… (AO3)

_____

_____

_____

_____

_____

_____

_____

_____

_____

_____

_____

_____

_____

_____

Psychological explanations of offending behaviour: Psychodynamic

Specification notes
Psychological explanations of offending behaviour: psychodynamic explanations.

Year 2
Student Book
Pages 272–273

---

1 Which **one** of the following does **not** feature in psychodynamic explanations of offending behaviour?

Tick **one** box only.

[1 mark]   AO1 = 1

A	Superego.	
B	Hostile attribution.	
C	Maternal deprivation.	
D	Affectionless psychopathy.	

 Topic link

You can find out more about the psychodynamic approach on page 134 of the Year 1 Student Book.

---

2 Evaluate psychodynamic explanations of offending behaviour.

[4 marks]   AO3 = 4

One strength of the psychodynamic approach is that it is the only explanation of offending that considers emotional factors.

For example, unlike cognitive theories, it takes into account _____

_____

It also recognises the role of innate drives and _____

_____

This means that _____

_____

---

3 Agnes found a wallet full of money lying on the pavement. At first, she thought, 'I'd better take this to the police station.' Then, she thought, 'No I won't. I'll go and buy myself some new clothes.' Even though she knew it was wrong, she spent the money on clothes. However, when she got home she bitterly regretted how she had behaved.

[4 marks]   AO2 = 4

Outline a psychodynamic explanation of Agnes' behaviour.

The superego is _____

This was the structure of the mind that meant Agnes _____

_____

The id is _____

It appears that Agnes has _____

_____

This is because _____

_____

 Exam tip

The question asks about 'Agnes', so you will only gain full marks if you apply your knowledge to **her** behaviour.

4 According to some psychodynamic psychologists, adult criminality is unconsciously motivated and sometimes due to repression of personality conflicts and unresolved problems experienced in early childhood. To support their claims, these psychologists rely extensively on case studies. However, psychodynamic hypotheses have been difficult to falsify when tested using objective empirical methods.

4(a)	[4 marks]	AO1 = 4
4(b)	[2 marks]	AO1 = 2
4(c)	[3 marks]	AO2 = 3

(a) What is a case study? Outline **one** limitation of using cases studies in psychological research.

_____

_____

_____

_____

(b) Explain what is meant by 'objectivity' as a feature of science.

_____

_____

(c) Falsifiability is an important feature of science. Explain why it is important that hypotheses derived from psychodynamic theories are falsifiable.

_____

_____

_____

⭐ **Exam tip**

Questions (b) and (c) come from a part of the specification that students often 'forget' to revise. Remember – if it's on the specification, it can be asked about in your exam.

---

5 Discuss psychodynamic explanations of offending behaviour.

[12 marks]	AO1 = 6	AO3 = 6
[16 marks]	AO1 = 6	AO3 = 10

The suggested paragraph starters below will help form your answer:

- Bowlby's maternal deprivation theory says that offending behaviour is the result of… (AO1)

- Freud's psychoanalytic theory says that… (AO1)

- This means offending behaviour is the result of… (AO1)

- One strength of Bowlby's theory is that it has important applications in the care of young children. For example… (AO3)

- However, one problem with Bowlby's research is that it only shows a correlation between separation and emotional problems. For example… (AO3)

- One problem with Freud's theory is that it is gender biased. For example… (AO3)

- One strength of psychodynamic explanations is that they are the only explanations of offending that consider emotional factors. For example… (AO3)

- One problem with psychodynamic explanations of offending behaviour is that they cannot explain all causes of offending. For example… (AO3)

_____

_____

_____

_____

_____

⭐ **Exam tip**

As only 6 marks are available for AO1, it is important to keep your description concise and to the point.

Dealing with offending behaviour: Custodial sentencing and recidivism

Specification notes
Dealing with offending behaviour: the aims of custodial sentencing and the psychological effects of custodial sentencing. Recidivism.

Year 2
Student Book
Pages 274–275

---

1 Which **one** of the following is **not** an aim of custodial sentencing?

[1 mark] | AO1 = 1

Tick **one** box only.

A	Encouraging recidivism.	
B	Deterring others from committing crime.	
C	Rehabilitating offenders.	
D	Protecting the public.	

---

2 Evaluate the psychological effects of custodial sentencing.

[4 marks] | AO3 = 4

One limitation of custodial sentencing is that prison may increase reoffending by acting as a training ground for crime.

Sutherland's differential association theory suggests that spending time with other criminals

will _____

_____

Also, Latessa and Lowenkamp found that _____

_____

This means that _____

_____

 Exam tip

As there are only 4 marks available, you can choose to make one evaluative point in more detail, or two evaluation points in less detail.

---

3 A research team was interested in the impact of prison education on recidivism. They measured the time reoffenders went before being convicted of another crime, and compared this with how many qualifications they had obtained during their time in prison. They found a significant correlation between the two measurements.

| 3(a) | [3 marks] | AO2 = 3 |
| 3(b) | [1 mark] | AO2 = 1 |

(a) Write a suitable non-directional hypothesis for this study.

_____

_____

_____

_____

(b) Name a statistical test that the researchers could have used to measure the relationship between the two variables.

_____

 Exam tip

Remember that a non-directional hypothesis predicts that there is a difference or correlation without stating the direction of the difference or correlation.

(c) When the researchers published their study, a television programme reported that the study showed that prison education leads to a reduction in reoffending. Explain why the television programme's interpretation of the study's results might be inappropriate.	3(c) **[3 marks]**	AO2 = 3

_____

_____

_____

4 Discuss custodial sentencing as a way of dealing with offending behaviour.	**[12 marks]**	AO1 = 6	AO3 = 6
	[16 marks]	AO1 = 6	AO3 = 10

The suggested paragraph starters below will help form your answer:

- The aims of custodial sentencing are… (AO1)

- There are psychological effects of custodial sentencing, including… (AO1)

- One problem with custodial sentencing is that incapacitation, retribution, and rehabilitation are not very beneficial. For example… (AO3)

- Another problem with custodial sentencing is that it is ineffective in preventing recidivism, or acting as a deterrent. For example… (AO3)

- A third problem with custodial sentencing is that it may increase reoffending, rather than reducing it. For example… (AO3)

- A fourth problem with custodial sentencing is that it may only be effective for some offenders. For example… (AO3)

- A final problem with custodial sentencing is that non-custodial sentencing may be more appropriate. For example… (AO3)

_____

_____

_____

_____

_____

_____

_____

_____

_____

_____

_____

_____

_____

_____

_____

_____

_____

Dealing with offending behaviour: Behaviour modification in custody

Specification notes
Dealing with offending behaviour: behaviour modification in custody.

Year 2
Student Book
Pages 276–277

---

1 Which **one** statement best describes how behaviour modification is used to deal with offending behaviour?

Tick **one** box only.

[1 mark]   AO1 = 1

A	It is used to increase or decrease the frequency of behaviour using operant conditioning.	
B	It is used to increase or decrease the frequency of behaviour using classical conditioning.	
C	It involves giving rewards for good behaviour.	
D	It involves offenders setting their own goals to improve behaviour.	

---

2 Explain **one** criticism of using behaviour modification as a way to deal with offender behaviour.

[4 marks]   AO3 = 4

Token economy systems do not affect reoffending rates outside the prison. This is because the

token economy only has short-term effects while _____

_____

Furthermore, the behaviours learned in prisons _____

_____

This means that _____

_____

Exam tip

Although the word 'explain' is used in this question, you are actually being asked to show your AO3 rather than your AO1 skills.

---

3 Ian was an uncooperative prison inmate, and refused to take part in any organised activities. The only thing prison officers knew about Ian was that he really liked seeing Liverpool play football. However, he couldn't do this in prison as the inmates were not allowed to watch television.

[4 marks]   AO2 = 4

Using information in the item above, outline how behaviour modification might be used to increase Ian's cooperativeness.

SAMPLE ANSWER: *Token economies aim to increase desirable, non-criminal behaviours. Tokens act as secondary reinforcers, and are given for behaving in desirable ways, such as obeying orders or taking part in organised activities. They can then be exchanged for primary reinforcers, which are desirable goods that the individual wants.*

This means that if Ian takes part in organised activities, then he will be given tokens, which can be exchanged for something he does like — watching Liverpool play football on the television.

④ A researcher wanted to use a token economy programme with offenders in a maximum security prison. Twenty offenders were randomly selected from an initial sixty who had volunteered to take part in the programme. The researcher identified four target behaviours, one of which was having a neat and well-groomed personal appearance. An offender was judged to have met this target if he was clean-shaven, if his hair was combed, and if his shirt was tucked into his trousers. The member of staff on duty scored each offender on a daily basis for the four target behaviours. Points were awarded each time a target behaviour was met, and these were exchanged at the end of the week for things like access to a television viewing room.

4(a)	[1 mark]	AO2 = 1	
4(b)	[3 marks]	AO1 = 2	AO2 = 1
4(c)	[3 marks]	AO2 = 3	
4(d)	[2 marks]	AO2 = 2	

(a) Suggest **one** other criterion the researchers could have used for the target behaviour of having a neat and well-groomed appearance.

_____

(b) Identify the sampling technique initially used by the researcher and outline **one** limitation of this sampling technique.

_____
_____
_____

Exam tip

The specification requires you to know about **five** sampling techniques. These are opportunity, random, stratified, systematic, and volunteer sampling.

(c) Briefly explain **one** way in which the researcher could have assessed the reliability of the staff member's judgements about whether the criteria for the target behaviours had been met.

_____
_____
_____

(d) Three days into the study, one of the offenders told the researcher that he no longer wanted to participate in it. Outline how the researcher should have dealt with this issue.

_____
_____

⑤ Discuss the use of behaviour modification in custody as a way to deal with offender behaviour.

[12 marks]	AO1 = 6	AO3 = 6
[16 marks]	AO1 = 6	AO3 = 10

The suggested paragraph starters below will help form your answer:

- The token economy system is based on… (AO1)

- It aims to… (AO1)

- It involves… (AO1)

- One strength of token economies is that they can be effective and easy to implement. For example… (AO3)

- However, one criticism of the token economy is that it is less successful in prisons than in schools. For example… (AO3)

- Another criticism of the token economy is that it doesn't affect reoffending rates, or behaviour outside the prison. For example… (AO3)

- A third criticism of the token economy is that it is not effective for all criminals. For example… (AO3)

- A final criticism of the token economy is that there are ethical issues with its use. For example… (AO3)

_____

Exam tip

'Discuss' is a command word which requires you to show both your AO1 and AO3 skills. You'll need to show your knowledge and understanding of how behaviour modification has been used **and** be able to evaluate its use as a way of dealing with offending behaviour.

Specification notes
Dealing with offending behaviour: anger management.

Year 2
Student Book
Pages 278–279

---

1 Which **one** of the following is **not** an aim of anger management in dealing with offender behaviour?

Tick **one** box only.

[1 mark] AO1 = 1

A	To rehabilitate offenders.	
B	To change the way offenders think about their behaviour in certain situations.	
C	To increase physiological arousal in response to provocation.	
D	To give offenders better communication skills.	

---

2 Evaluate anger management programmes as a way to deal with offender behaviour.

[4 marks] AO3 = 4

One limitation of anger management programmes is that they assume that treating anger will reduce aggression and violent crime.

However, Loza and Loza-Fanous found _____

_____

This may be because _____

_____

This suggests that _____

_____

Exam tip

You do not have to write about a limitation of anger management. Writing about a strength will also receive AO3 credit.

---

3 A researcher wanted to study the effectiveness of an anger management technique she had devised. She used a questionnaire to provide her with a baseline measure of anger in 40 offenders. The offenders were then randomly allocated to either a control group who did not receive the technique or an experimental group who did. Two months later, the same questionnaire was used to take a second measure of anger.

3(a)	[2 marks]	AO3 = 2	
3(b)	[3 marks]	AO2 = 1	AO3 = 2

(a) Explain **one** limitation of using a self-report technique to measure anger.

_____

_____

_____

(b) Identify the experimental design used in this study, and outline **one** limitation of this experimental design.

_____

_____

_____

_____

Exam tip

Think about the extent to which the design used controls for participant variables.

(c) Explain why a control group was necessary for the study described in the item above.	**3(c)** **[3 marks]**	AO2 = 3

_____

_____

_____

_____

4 Outline and evaluate anger management programmes as a way of dealing with offender behaviour.	**[12 marks]**	AO1 = 6	AO3 = 6
	[16 marks]	AO1 = 6	AO3 = 10

The suggested paragraph starters below will help form your answer:

- Anger management programmes use a cognitive approach to change… (AO1)

- Cognitive therapy accepts the situation itself may not change, but it is possible to change… (AO1)

- Anger management programmes focus on cognitive restructuring, which is… (AO1)

- They also focus on the regulation of arousal, which is… (AO1)

- A third focus is on behaviour strategies, such as… (AO1)

- One strength of anger management programmes is that they are successful in reducing anger. For example, Taylor and Novaco… (AO3)

- However, one problem with anger management programmes is that studies investigating their effectiveness are difficult to compare. For example… (AO3)

- Another problem is that most studies only look at the short-term goals of reducing anger in prisons. For example… (AO3)

- A third problem with anger management programmes is that many offenders drop out of the programmes. This may be because… (AO3)

- A final problem with anger management programmes is that they assume that treating anger will reduce aggression and violent crime. For example… (AO3)

> ★ **Exam tip**
>
> You could also evaluate anger management techniques by comparing them with other ways of dealing with offending behaviour. Are they, for example, more or less effective than other techniques?

_____

_____

_____

_____

_____

_____

_____

_____

_____

_____

_____

_____

_____

_____

_____

Dealing with offending behaviour: Restorative justice programmes

Specification notes
Dealing with offending behaviour: restorative justice programmes.

Year 2
Student Book
Pages 280–281

---

1 Which **one** of the following is a feature of restorative justice?

[1 mark] | AO1 = 1

Tick **one** box only.

A	It always involves communication between the offender and the victim.	
B	It is offered as an alternative to prison even if the victim disagrees.	
C	It encourages offenders to take responsibility for their crimes.	
D	It never involves a face-to-face meeting between the offender and the victim.	

---

2 Outline what is involved in a restorative justice programme.

[4 marks] | AO1 = 4

The victim explains the impact of the crime, so that _____
_____

Offenders will offer _____
_____

As the victim has a voice, they _____
_____

Exam tip

Remember that 'Outline' questions are AO1 only.

---

3 A team of researchers wanted to study a restorative justice programme they had devised. Offenders taking part in the programme were asked various open-ended questions. For example, they were asked what they wanted to gain from the programme, and whether they thought it would be likely to deter them from committing crime. Thematic analysis was used to derive themes in the offenders' responses, and the researchers calculated the frequencies for each of the themes that emerged.

3(a) | [4 marks] | AO2 = 4
3(b) | [1 mark] | AO2 = 1

(a) Identify the quantitative and qualitative data collected in the researchers' study. Explain your answer.

_____
_____
_____
_____
_____

Exam tip

Remember that qualitative data is information in words that cannot be counted or quantified.

(b) Name an appropriate measure of central tendency that could be used in this study.

_____

(c) Outline **one** strength and **one** limitation of using thematic analysis in psychological research.

3(c)	**[4 marks]**	AO3 = 4

_____

_____

_____

_____

_____

[12 marks]	AO1 = 6	AO3 = 6
[16 marks]	AO1 = 6	AO3 = 10

4 Discuss restorative justice programmes.

The suggested paragraph starters below will help form your answer:

- Restorative justice enables offenders to… (AO1)

- It aims to… (AO1)

- It does this by… (AO1)

- One strength of these programmes is that they do reduce reoffending rates. For example, Sherman and Strang… (AO3)

- Another strength of restorative justice programmes is that they are more beneficial than custodial sentencing. For example… (AO3)

- A third strength of restorative justice programmes is that there is research evidence that victims find it beneficial. For example… (AO3)

- However, one limitation of restorative justice programmes is that the victim may feel worse afterwards. For example… (AO3)

- Another limitation of restorative justice programmes is that they aren't appropriate for all types of crime. For example… (AO3)

 Exam tip

Using research findings is an excellent way of evaluating the strengths and weaknesses of any approach to dealing with offending behaviour.

_____

_____

_____

_____

_____

_____

_____

_____

_____

_____

_____

_____

_____

_____

_____

The Complete Companions
Psychology A Level Paper 3

Authors
Clare Compton, Rob McIlveen

Series Editor
Mike Cardwell

From the team that brought you the best-selling and trusted *The Complete Companions*, *The Complete Companions Exam Workbooks* provide students with skills-building activities and step-by-step exam-style practice questions to ensure they approach their exams confident of success. They are completely matched to AQA's AS and A Level examination requirements and ideal for use in class or for homework and revision.

This *A Level Paper 3 Exam Workbook* covers **Forensic psychology**, one of the optional topics examined by A Level Paper 3.

- Perfect for use with the AQA Psychology specification from 2019 onwards, so you can trust that you've covered everything you need to practise.

- Draws on **key issues from examiner reports**, so you can be confident that it reflects exactly what is required for success at both AS and A Level.

- Focussed **exam advice and tips** throughout, with suggested **AO1/AO2/AO3 mark allocations** to help structure answers.

Also available:

Paper 1 Exam Workbook for AQA
978-019-842890-9

Paper 2 Exam Workbook for AQA
978-019-842891-6

Paper 3 Exam Workbook for AQA: Relationships including Issues and debates
978-019-842895-4

Paper 3 Exam Workbook for AQA: Gender including Issues and debates
978-019-842894-7

Paper 3 Exam Workbook for AQA: Aggression
978-019-842892-3

Paper 3 Exam Workbook for AQA: Schizophrenia
978-019-842896-1

Exam-style practice questions for each topic, ramped from lower tariff to essay style

Marks clearly presented with suggested breakdown of Assessment Objectives

Tips and guidance based on key issues raised in examiner reports

Essential for A Level students, with guidance to help deliver the greater depth required to achieve top grades

Answers can be found at www.oxfordsecondary.co.uk/completecompanionsanswers

OXFORD
UNIVERSITY PRESS

How to get in touch:
web   www.oxfordsecondary.co.uk
email schools.enquiries.uk@oup.com
tel   01536 452620

ISBN 978-0-19-842893-0